True Fan

Real Life Poetry

True Fan

Real Life Poetry

De'Broada Cornelius

iCreativ Books

Kansas

iCreativ Books
an imprint of iCreativ Properti, LLC.
6505 E. Central Suite #314,
Wichita KS 67206

Printed in the United States of America.

True Fan: Real Life Poetry
ISBN: 978-0-692-97663-0

iCreativ Books
6505 E. Central Suite #314,
Wichita KS 67206
www.icreativproperti.com

True Fan...this is for you

Thank you for reading.

Poetry helps us because it tells the story of emotion. Every day we make choices and create outcomes that help us make sense about the world—the beauty and ugliness. For the most part, we're figuring things out and learn many lessons the hard way.

All experiences are worthy of creative expression, and the gift of language gives voice to the emotions that reveal the perceptions of our heart-mind and often the gateway is diverse, naked, wet and rich—poetic. For me, poetry, empathetically helps make the point that everyone is in the process of interpreting life.

What you're reading.

True Fan, Real Life Poetry, is a collection of poems about real life situations and conversations—the good, bad, happy and sad. Poetry conveys different messages to the reader. Being so, the language of oral art is allowed to fulfill its purpose. Read and experience for yourself. I'm a "true fan" of poetry and a true fan of you...I have to stay true to make my dreams come true. Stay connected.

De'Broada

db@icreativproperti.com

Contents

I
Struggle

II
Love & Pain

III
Seasons

1
<u>Struggle</u>

You'll never live a life where you never offend anyone. So, practice doing what you're good at.

The Church Lady

She said to me, "You never gave up, you never quit." Her words ran through me like water rushing, gushing. I couldn't believe what I was hearing. Someone, not someone, "she" had been paying attention to what I loved to do and was proud of me. It felt good. It felt good to be understood.

"The presence of struggle does not indicate the failure to advance—keep moving." -Unknown

A man's steps are directed by the Lord. How then can anyone understand his own way? ~Proverbs

Strugglin'

I'm strugglin'
Been strugglin'
Was born in struggle
It's really a *%$#! up sight to see
Reality keeps a choke hold on me
This writing better set me free
I'm dangling between
Anger and anxiety
I believe in what I write
I believe in me
This writing better set me free
Slow and steady is my pace
Slow and steady wins the race
This writing better set me free
Struggling isn't the place for me
I believe in what I write
I believe in me
This writing better set me free

People Poetry

Read what's here
Don't skip one line
Don't look for good stuff
This ain't a nursery rhyme
Its poetry for people
What I see
Family, trees, genealogy
Linage and stories
Between you and me
Like it or not—history
Choose not to care
Every line written will lead you here
Your decision I can't change
Nor, will I try
Poetry for people
You know your why
Unconventional capitalization
Messed up punctuation
Conversations and situations
Intentional confrontation
Experience expressed
Unaltered from divine
Exact as exact—line as line
Come into being people poetry
I "be" seeing

Read, feed, soothe needs
Balance doesn't exist between love and greed
Never get enough like the grave and trust
Poetry for people just like us

Alone

Alone with my words
Wondering if they'll be heard
Some thoughts sound absurd
Alone with my words
Mozart's art silence of Beethoven
Some say heaven isn't open
So, is this hell?
All I know is…
Words can place you under a spell
If you let 'em
I believed in love
Love didn't believe in me
I spilled my cup
It became poetry
But you didn't hear me
Morning comes
So, will the Son
Moonlight ends
One trip around the sun
Alone with my words
Come out of your cage
Reasons equal seasons
Turn the page

Gift

Sometimes I write in my draaws'
I write for a cause
I write in the bath
I write to make you laugh
I write cause I'm deep
'Cause I can't sleep
When I want to yell
Got a story to tell
I write cause I'm mad
When I feel bad
I write to offend
With a message to send
I don't know why
I do what I do
Just know I'm doing
What I'm 'sposed to
I write what I see
Instructed by thee
Exposing free verse
Natural rhythms of speech
If you listen you can teach
Transcend, transmit, translate
Communicate, educate, penetrate
Imitate, motivate, demonstrate
Situate myself in your time

Help you find sameness of mind
Self operates to separate
Spirit from thee
There's a message here
Can you hear me?
No fear, move near
Embrace and behold
Memory of a shadow's soul
For we are the story left untold
Left behind but through grace
Reconnected and infected with familiarity
Not wanting to believe what we see
We are the energy of His chemistry
Sometimes I write in my draaws'
I write for a cause
I write in the bath
I write to make you laugh
I write cos I'm deep
'Cause I can't sleep
When I want to yell
Got a story to tell
I write cause I'm mad
When I feel bad
I write to offend
With a message to send
I don't know why I do what I do
Just know I'm doing what I'm 'sposed to

For Purpose

How do I wish to use my life?
As a vehicle for whatever comes to mind
mind of programmed illusions
mixed with words, thought creates confusion
I live by which I die trying to become
to express the energy, I feel
at the expense of free will and the intellect
a testimony from the apple tree
providing supplication, damnation in one swoop
let me shoot a hoop and fly this coop
of captivity
to "be" is not free
it cost to find a lost soul I've been told
by the old man of the dam
and the slaughtered lamb −of sacrifice
who didn't think twice
about paying the price of eternal life
this temporary state I await
a return of investment on faith
don't haste or, waste any more time
inside you'll find the mind
has the authority to do most things
so, it seems
devising schemes, creating teams of externals
comfort keepers, walkers, sleepers

eyes wide shut, living in a rut
depressions confession boil emotions
in an ocean of detachment, not heaven sent
we better repent, for purpose we all were sent

Howling Spirit

So unsettled
Words dripping off my brain
Taking me in places
Spaces of the sane
Riding on a train
Smelling rain
Sound drip from my lips
Into penmanship
I grip to complete a volume of script
Words caught, who lends an ear?
Understand truth of what you hear
Voice inside speak out loud
Something trying to drown sound
Monkey brain does not know
How low you'll stoop for Ego
Senses create fake control
Boundaries hold willing souls
Until death comes
She ends the beginning
Howling spirit, no one is winning
Another time…another place
Alter space, separate from grace
Into the abyss pray I miss
Opportunity of eating from the apple tree
And falling from thee…save me

Mutation

Forgive dishonor and disrespect
Lame excuses and fear of reject
It's about you n' me in this game
Agreement made before I came
To this place called "whirl"
Planet of fools
Hell, damnation—Satan's tools
Lift my head I must see through
Keep my mind focused on true
Serving I am, not opinions I see
Ruined mind falls into complacency
All pressure comes from sin
I do what I do not want, and do it again
Exercise willpower change direction
Get this load off me
Resistance causes infection
An open mouth tells what mind see
Many need a word given me
Loaded before age of accountability
Repeated mistakes destroy society
Resentful events need no validation
Disease of mind called mutation

No Dress Code

Don't ask me nothing personal
I don't want to tell you a lie
But I will
Depends on how I feel
Just being real...trying to heal
Not forced, coerced, nursed or, churched
Think it over, don't call me friend
Know it is I, within there is sin
Look for me, I am in you
Face your fears see what's true
Forget desire we're from all there is
All that can be, all that lives
Channel of infinite potentiality
Resist impulse you'll hear me
Be the challenges you seek
Enter doors don't retreat
Abundantly open more than good
Nothing looks as you think it should
Step into you there's no dress code
Don't expect good until you unload
Expose yourself as meant to be
Or, remain naked in shame of what the "I" see

Alibis

Keep waiting
Something's gonna change it
Keep hoping
Magic will rearrange it
Just sit on the matter
There's no way you'll lose
Bump what they say
You don't have to choose
Everything's all worked out
It's your luck that's so bad
Mom was okay
But, if you had a different dad
No, it wasn't dad
It was 'cause you were poor
And the neighborhood boys
Who taught you to whore
Knowing right from wrong
Self-pity is easy to express
It gets so much attention
Settles anger's unrest
If, I would've been prettier
And had long hair
If, I wouldn't have gotten pregnant
And had someone to care
If, I wasn't weak and unfocused

Valuing others more than I
If, I didn't argue with the enemy
Every morning until I cry
If, I applied love bandages
Over wounds of self-hate
I wouldn't make excuses and tell lies
I wouldn't need all these alibis

Impulse

Follow your hunches
They hit like punches
And come in bunches
If you listen

Filter

I was off kilter
So, I ran my filter
The litter was bitter
That's when I saw the quitter
In me

Interrupted

Why I got a problem with being free?
That's where I say I wanna be
I got a problem 'cause I ain't use to it
I got a problem 'cause it's harder to do it
To just let go…feel the high
Let people see the color of my sky
Only judge is the critic within
Suffering caused by one's own sin
Go to work day after day
Pretend that's where I want to be
Wondering when is it gonna end
Cries of self-misery
Purge my fears
Smile and lie to self
Distribute out the "me" that's left
Intuition says this is not God's plan
Practiced faith is stronger in man
Why I got a problem with being free?
Been depending on man instead of thee

People's Anthem

If I didn't love money or, material things
I wouldn't be here, I wouldn't be here
If I wasn't a slave to pleasure
—gratification of the external
I wouldn't be here, I wouldn't be here
Forbidden fruit I've been given
To have remained in the garden
And experienced the living
If I could embrace the unknown
With the arrogant confidence
I have when I breathe
I wouldn't be here
No loyalty have I in this place
Hypnotic, robotic process of being
"Operation Gratification" the penalty of seeing
Subconsciously this game I deconstruct
Through conditional bondage and repetition
Freedom has been took
I feel stuck
I wouldn't be here if I wasn't stuck in fear
I wouldn't be here if I wasn't stuck in fear
I wouldn't be here if I wasn't stuck in fear
Look at us, all running around
Quite aware of what's going down
Chasing something called goals

Redefining ourselves
By the encrypted code of self-righteousness
The concept of slavery has never changed
There's the slave and the master
The master and the slave
Subconsciously this game I deconstruct
Through conditional bondage and repetition
Freedom has been took
We are stuck
We wouldn't be here, if we weren't stuck in fear
We wouldn't be here if we weren't stuck in fear
We wouldn't be here if we weren't stuck in fear
Divine discontent with this experiment
The purpose for which we've been sent
Invisible warfare the most destructive kind
Powers and principalities seek control of mind
Subconsciously this game I deconstruct
Through conditional bondage and repetition
Freedom has been took
We are stuck
We wouldn't be here if we weren't stuck in fear
We wouldn't be here if we weren't stuck in fear
We wouldn't be here if we weren't stuck in fear

Pause

There's a pause in blackness
That bothers me
A space that changes
The pace of destiny
Why?
There's a pause in white
That doesn't seem right
A space that changes
An interruption of sight
Why?

Blueprint of Alpha

Etched in my soul, I came from you
You were my first love, first kiss, first view
Early breaks of the heart
Still remember the first two
Refused to give up—see I came from you
Yet, you watch me walk by, sit alone
Watch me cry and make it on my own
You deserve me the throne is for two
Molding the seeds of your source
Again, I came from you
Blueprint of Alpha, the world is our due
No longer can I live in the shadow of you
Etched in my soul, a queen's love is true
Yet, left all alone trying to raise you
Etched, etched, etched
In my soul, soul, soul
I came, came, came
From you, you, you

Accident / Evidence

Say it was an accident
How could it have been meant?
The man said...get that gun out of my face
Rather than being disgraced
Death set the pace of trigger control
Even though the barrel he did hold
Death got two for one that day on stage
The accused was only 14 years of age
But he said... it was an accident
Spreading his legs, he cocked the trigger
He meant to shoot him the way that I figure
The accident was the consequence of being caught
A soul being bought
Let me explain
The accident was... the consequence of being caught
A soul being bought
Paying the cost, a life being lost
The parental consent of too much TV
Laughing at evil, a sleeping society brutality
Generations so aloof and removed from truth
It shows first in our youth
Being caught on tape while trying to escape
A chosen fate, now called mistake
The time spent prior to the incident
Daydreams of being well known for something ignorant

Five minutes of fame everybody knows his name
Not thinking in time of the family left behind
The hostile environment where educators teach
Children sent by parents whom they have not reached
The media being content gathering evidence
Arguing over the intent of loss innocence
Seeing life through carnal eyes and living
institutionalized
Of course, he ran
Demons always flee
Leaving our Judas to hang
From the consequence tree
Spreading his legs, he cocked the trigger
He meant to kill him he was just another nigger
It was no accident
It was evidence
Proof of a lack of common sense
Of concentration and communication
Wrapped in apathy and frustration
The birth of life incarceration
The suicide of freedom and mentality
The suicide of freedom and mentality
Of we all came to die its either you or me?
Serving the self, knowing no God
To fear, hear or be near
As the plot is revealed
Life doesn't appeal
To those unaware

Of their fill of spirit
So, we run amok and self-destruct
The accident is that everything is instant
In a minute, in a flash, internet
How we forget to participate
So, we underestimate
Our gift of life… of breath
The bullet exited his chest and came to rest
On the consciousness of a minor
Mine or, your child saying it was an accident
Spreading his legs, he cocked the trigger
Second amendment rights protected another killer
The loss of life is bigger than our Constitution
Arrested development is not the solution

Trip Mind

I find a quiet space and try to erase
all that has happened, that I can remember
then my mind goes black and back
and back and black to a time
when yours was mine
and I used to see you
it was like I knew you
man…, it took so long
for them to sing our song
Marvin Gaye and Louis Armstrong
and I think to myself, What A Wonderful World
then my mind goes back and black
and black and back and I'm wondering
how can you trust a system
that gave birth to Jim Crow
and using the back-doe?
a standard of beauty of Marilyn Monroe
I don't know, but I need to confess
capitalism is fascism at its best
now, I understand how mama and daddy's stress
can you hear the connection of words?
my rhythm of prose wants to expose
and explode back into that space so, I can erase
all that has happened, that I can remember
Then my mind goes black and back

And back and black, to a time
When me and my girl use to drank wine
Laugh loud looking for a reason to clown
and some heavy conversation to wrap our minds around
Yeah, now we got babies and life ain't no gravy
'cos it's so much shit to do
you could lose you in the process
of other people's progress
got me feeling stressed
caught in my own mess
again, I must confess
welfare is institutionalized poverty at its best
now, I understand Shaniqua and Keisha's helplessness
that's why I want my space, so, I can erase
all that has happened, that I can remember
then my mind goes black and back
I'm under attack
not my mind…my spirit
listen, hear it?
fear, ego, fits of anger
hazard to myself…a walking danger
always fighting for freedom and fearing arrest
looking for the mark of the beast
is my daily test
that's why I want my space
so, I can erase
all that has happened
then my mind goes black

and I'm back here with you
and I realize… damn, I chose this

Pardon Me

Its early
Truth is in my face
Ready, wanting, new change of pace
Quickly affected negatively
Lord, help myself, help me, help me
Past creeped up, wouldn't let it speak
Gagged its mouth like slaughtered sheep
Disguised mind shadows tuned in again
Check your thoughts I'm not your friend
You may not recall but, I surely do
Disposed me like garbage I didn't know what to do
Took a long time wasted hate on you
Like debt you made the list of regret
I refurbished my mind—autocorrect
Be gone fool hope failure you've found
No longer in my head no time for clowns
My highest thought I must stay true
Work on dreams I see in view
I like early
Truth is in my face
Finally created my change of pace

Idle Time

Idle time
Messing with my baby's mind
Trying hard as hell
To teach him to excel
I sit around and think
Pour me a drink
I don't even yell anymore
Tell me again
What are we waiting for?

Shut Up

From the horse's mouth
Comes the ass
Starting with judgment
Of one's past
Selectively forgetting
How it works
Shut up, shut up
Shut up, shut up

You Are

You Are what you eat
Things lead to things
Stop while you're ahead
How many pieces of that bread
Are you going to eat?
Treat yourself too
One pound or two
Feel your hunger
Its satisfied
Release the urge
Of gluttony's pride
Why eat more than you need or, desire
Eat until your stomach and jowls tire
Things lead to things

Monkey Brain

Monkey brain, donkey breath
Will put hypertext to the test
Got negative talk going through my head
Negative talk all in my dreads
Every move I make it wants to be fed
Got negative talk going through my head
Telling me what I can't be, see, why can't we
Every sound smells funky to me
Trying to get in looking for a friend
Creeping, seeking space in mind
Arresting peace capturing divine
Plotting, planning, scheming, scamming
Trying to make ill of God's will
Will to flow with all you know
Process the process of letting go
Got negative talk going through my head
Negative talk going through my head
Every move I make it wants to be fed
Got negative talk going through my head
Get out of my head!

You Know

Things are things
Stuff is stuff
You got to know when
You've had enough
You do, but you don't
No self-respect
You lack control
Believe you can hold
Pain of ego
Said you could
But not doing good
Living toxicity, you know
Want radical change
But refuse to grow
Doing the easy
Making life hard
Contribute to madness
Calling on God
Things are things
Stuff is stuff
You know when
You've had enough

Focus

I put my attention
On the wrong thing today
It messed with my juice,
My flow, what I know
I couldn't let it grow
But it did slow me down
I turned it over n' over in mind
A few times more than I needed too
Not, that I wanted to control the view
I just didn't pay attention to
What I paid attention too
Not doing so, took me to places, spaces
Waste of grace, time and energy
What I'm saying is, I let someone get to me
Truth is, it doesn't matter
Not something I care to affect
Just the waste of God's gift is what I regret
Stay on course!

Stolen Moments

Sometimes
The most precious moments
Are missed
With the...
I'll call you right back
When the only time we have is now

My Way

We do a good job of running off the road
But, a better job of running others off
When they don't behave
The way we want them to
She's not going to do
What you want her to
Just like you're not
He's focused on his needs
Working to keep himself happy
We do a good job of running off the road
But a better job of running others off

Speeches

My stuff wasn't good enough
I didn't know what to say
My stuff wasn't good enough
I had to kneel down and pray
Lord, help me craft this piece
For, still in bed I lay
Lord, help me craft this piece
To them what do you want me to say?
Stroke my thoughts nourish my words
For your purpose I've asked to be heard
Tell them...
I am here, no matter what you believe
Take heed, do not be troubled
Nor, let your heart be deceived
Don't believe in perception
Or, get lost in your feelings
For, I am the Resurrection
I hold your peace and your healing
For, the Lord is your shepherd
Is the Lord your shepherd?
Take a look at what God made
Tell me, how do you see yourself?
Take a look at what God made
Not what you think is left
From, where does your chaos come?
Why is it you cannot cope?

With what have you filled your mind
He's more than the strategy of hope
The rolling away of the stone
See, the place where he laid
Don't be afraid, believe the comfort of truth
He has risen from the grave
Satan hasn't taken a day off, he bears a witness too
Listen to me, hear what I say
The decision to believe rest on you
Every day, is Resurrection Day
Somebody's going die tonight
The opportunity for salvation is now
Take the time get your life right
There are days… when you hate your life
What hasn't he done for you?
Listen within, hear your thoughts
Tell me…is that lie true?
Unbelief is a pattern, a practiced lie
For, the Lord God does not change
Align yourself with the spirit He left
Get on the higher plain
My soul doesn't yield to logical examination
Nor, can my mind pin down my spirit
I respond to the energy placed in me
It's not my fault if you can't hear it
He brought me out of the shadows
I found my way back to me
My soul has been resurrected

My spirit he has set free
I stand upon my fears,
He placed them under my feet
This is the right space, place and time
Listen, tune in as I speak
For, words are the service I offer to you
They're filled with the purpose to teach
For, those of you listening, but cannot hear
Call this your Easter speech
My stuff isn't good enough
I didn't know what to say
Our stuff isn't good enough
We must kneel down and pray

Prom

Is black love different than any other love?
I pondered, as I queried the one from above
Trying to place color on something divine
Is like capturing the wind or, stopping time
This cannot be done
Love has no color and love is divine
Color creates perception
Correct the error in your mind
Love is not divided
Division is a tool of man
For there's only one power, presence and one plan
So, I said...
I've been asked to speak at the PROM
Celebrating love where two have become one
The voice said…
Words are the medium you will use to define
For the gift of marriage comes from the One mind
Everything is beautiful and one of a kind
The blessing of marriage is as old as time
This gift is not an "IF"
It's been given to you
The power of his presence
His energy flowing through
From two to one is the situation
But this is much more than a PROM celebration

For, you must be a steward over your love
I silenced my mind and said tell me more...
Silver and gold, have I none
The covenant of marriage
Where two become one
This gift is one of appreciation
Commitment, honor and dedication
Spirit of God sets things in motion
Hunger for your union builds trust and devotion
PROM
Prepare to receive other's mess (PROM)
This is what you meant when you said yes
There are negative seeds called expectation
Don't let this hinder your communication
For many things won't go your way
And you may not like what the other has to say
PROM
Promise to remain open and mature (PROM)
Continue to be faithful even when unsure
The language of argument
Keep far from its speech
For, what you learn you shall also teach
Opposition creates resentment and fear
Seek the voice of spirit keep the Word near
PROM
Pray, repent and obey the master (PROM)
Protect your union from self-made disaster
Wrong use of emotion builds walls and fences

The onset of unrelenting consequences
For you must be a steward over your love
Silver and gold, have I none
The covenant of marriage two become one
This is not a gift of equality
It's a sacrificial bond of unity
A lasting gift through all times and seasons
If indifference is nurtured
Ego is the reason
Error in your mind you are free to choose
With freedom comes responsibility
Don't abandon the rules
For, obedience brings blessing
Disobedience the curse of death
These are words of the spirit
Deuteronomy 30 says it best
He will not intervene
Without the request of two
Honor the commitment you've agreed too
The gift of marriage comes at a high cost
Forgive transgressions not to get lost
For, you must be a steward over your love
Celebrate your PROM and seek to understand
The plan of perfect peace between woman and man
For, love has many seasons
Appreciate every day the gift came to stay
And never forget the reasons
Silver and gold, have I none

United minds the two are one
Love has no color, love is divine
The opportunity for love is a brief moment in time
Love is not divided, division is a tool of man
For there's only one power, presence and one plan

Buried

I buried my life
Wanted it back
Didn't realize
It was a self-attack
Couldn't retract
All I'd done
Respect of my name
Crest of shame
Now my family holds the stain

Self-care

I let go of me, I don't know why
I didn't water my own leaves
I turned right and I know why
I just wasn't expecting my trees to die

Work Constitution

Got up this morning
Put on my face
Slipped into the world
Taking for granite God's grace
Started listening to stuff
Poisoned my mind
Caffeinated my spirit
Showed up on time
Continued the cycle
Of madness sadness
Keep the illusion alive
Monitor the chaos
Behind the truth I hide
Eight to ten hours robotic process for pay
Is how I spend the bulk of my day
Just a messenger at best
Adam's not at rest, there is no test
Only war
Not a fight, there is no right
Judas knew that night
Just war
The good news
I'm still in Adam's shoes
Know something about the blues
Still at war

Communication

Is not
Looking mad walking around sad
Wishing someone could change
Your bad to glad
Is not
Moving slow pretending
You don't know
Not letting go
Living in frustration making faces
Creating spaces in between
Wanting to escape and not be part of the scene
You chose to create
Living between not ready and wait
This is hesitation not communication
Do better

Battleground

I discount your words
Like pebbles on the roadside
For granted I take and make you mine
Altering signs along your journey
Who understands
Power of woman over man
When he's in love
With that created to compliment
—resent his way
Night cannot survive without day
And neither can our love
Balance we must achieve
Or, prepare to bereave and grieve
Over this mess
—battleground of consciousness
In which we seek to rest
The issues of our love

I Wanna

But, but, but
So, indecisive
Me, I can't trust
Be selfish
Learn to identify what best for you
Who else, who else are you listening to?
Can you stop yourself before you start?
Being reactive is not so smart
There's no magic but, miracles exist
It happens when you choose not to resist
All answers are waiting, waiting for you
Lined up to assist…what do you want to do?
Believe in the power of asking for
It's really okay to want more
Live your life

Assimilated

I hated her voice
She had no choice
She was an old educator
Assimilated through articulating
Perfecting words
Always did her part
To make sure she sounded smart
This wasn't art
I know what I hear
Practiced articulation during a time of fear
But, that was her time trying to change the mind
Of those who saw the color of her skin
To sound dumb was never fun
So, she fixed what she could
And became good
Eloquently articulating
Integrating and assimilating
And they still saw the color of her skin

Church Sista

No tape on my mouth
No cotton in my ear
Cussing is the only language
Some people understand my dear
You don't have to like it
The message isn't for you
Back in the day
You wuz cussing too
Get off yo' stoop
Ole' judgmental bag
Stating scripture like a prescription
Take time while carrying the cross
Look within you're still lost
Taming the tongue
Is a challenge for all
More than a four-letter word
Preceded Adam's fall
Remember your past
You came this way
Somebody had to reach
And teach you how to pray
Where is your focus?
Ole' bright star
Open your mind
We're still at war

Wonder Why?

I fell for the hook
She asked for the book
Looked good in the pic we took
Smooth not quite a crook
She was good
Never reached back
I fell for her act
No such thing like contact
That's how things go
Adjust high and low
Game of trying to get in
Not looking for friends
Have my own ends
Every shot blocked
Begin again
Starting from the end
Like scratch scribble scrabble
I dibble dabble—in and out
Wonder what this is all about
She looked, took the book
I fell for the hook
Thought something big
Was about to happen
It did
She never looked back

Cycles

C'mon Lord, why take so long?
Know you got things to do
And manage the throne
But I'm so "effing" frustrated
Why am I still waiting?
Mine
I just want mine
I just want mine
It
This ain't it
This ain't it
Me
Give it to me
Give it to me
All this waiting
Is too frustrating
I'm out...I'm gone
Wait, what do you mean follow my heart
If that's the answer where do I start?
C'mon Lord, why take so long?
Tell me what to do before I'm gone

Brainiac

Brain swims
Pool of words
Slow down whirlwind
Thought needs to be heard
On the next level
Much more aware
Understand pace
Just can't get you there
Keep up

Self-Doubt

Areas of weakness I possess
Periods of inconsistency
I don't do my best
Lack of concentration I digress
And, I'm mad about it
I want help
There's no power from without
I must believe in myself
To overcome self-doubt

Funny

I don't match the image
held in your mind
You labeled it
I disabled it
Funny

Perhaps

If you'd listen to understand
Instead of to respond
Maybe you'd experience
A different outcome

White Man

I've been segregated, discriminated
But never eliminated
Because I am Woman Warrior
Eyes that shine
Even though they've been shown darkness
Abuse, misuse, crime and hard time
You see strength in my face
But call it anger
Intimidated by something that's not there
You hear passion in my voice
And prepare for danger
When only there's the presence of air
With you I don't really have a choice
'Cause you've labeled me to silence my voice
But, you can't
Because, I am Woman Warrior
Eyes that shine
Even though they've been shown darkness
Abuse, misuse, crime and hard time
You can't place me on a shelf
Of items to be left
Because you're afraid of my hue
White man, what have I done to you?
Covered me with stereotypical lies
You fear the beauty behind my eyes
Because I am Woman Warrior

Differences

There's a difference between
Community and Colony
Bible and Constitution
This is why
Your problem is not the solution
Know the difference

Segregate

It may sound simple and simple is true
I didn't know I needed to love you too
I knew winter was cold and rain was wet
But loving you, how'd I forget?
I forgot 'cause all I could see was me, me
What I wanted and needed and needed and wanted
Lost in identity, I couldn't attach myself to you
The segregation in my mind revealed prejudices too
So, I walked the line of discriminating against you
It may sound simple and simple is true
I didn't know I needed to love you too
I knew winter was cold and rain was wet
But loving you how'd I forget?
I forgot 'cause pride is arrogant and arrogance is blind
I forgot that love is patient, love is kind
So, I didn't walk in the park, talk in the dark to you
I neglected, corrected, suspected and subjected you
And, you protected and respected me
'Cause I was all you knew
And you knew I needed to be loved too
The segregation in my mind is the defining line
Of why we aren't a two
The caste system has taught me there's a majority
And a minority and that changes the value of you
So, it may sound simple and simple is true

You really wanted me to love you too?
I knew winter was cold and rain was wet
But loving you how'd I forget?
I forgot 'cause nobody's seen Jesus or, been to Mars
'Cause sometimes fear is stronger than faith
'Cause they killed Dr. King, beat Rodney King
And drug James Byrd because of race
So, loving you wasn't an option
It was a risk
Entering the Wall Street of my mind
Divided by the invisible lines
Of involuntary membership with my kind
Again, segregation taught me to forget
And what I forget I neglect
And what I neglect I reject
And what I reject I object
And what I object I disrespect
So, it may sound simple and simple is true
I never thought of loving you
I didn't think...
'Cause a love like ours has so much in between
Babylon, KKK, lynching, Holocaust, 911, Ferguson
—the killing of one's dream
Social system, classes, colonialism of trained minds
Divided and exposed by God's loving and time
Needs to be redefined
Genocide resides in the illusion fear
Separated by sin my mind stood wanting to hear...

To understand…How am I supposed to love you?
Begin with the ending in mind
Not choosing the place but choosing the time
I choose to love you and you choose to love me
If were sister and brother
Why are we so terrible to one another?
It may sound simple and simple is true
Love is the answer so, what are you going to do?

Sittin'

Here I sit
Disconnect notice in hand
Trying to convince myself
This is part of God's plan—too suffer
Like Christ
To walk in a world filled with things
Not be affected by part of the scene
I'm human
Emotions stay on the very tip
Sedate my mind with caffeine I sip
Watching life happen
In the perpetual sense
Hearing sounds while passing time
As I head to stand in the bill paying line
Is this how he wanted it to be?
All resources exploited and the slavery...
Price tag on air and the water we drink
Rationed amount flows into my sink
Through pipes I pay taxes on
Did man make water?
Here I sit
Disconnect notice in hand
Trying to convince myself
This is part of God's plan—too suffer

Sittin' Still

Here I sit
Wishing you would
Work on your shit
But you can't
Because you're judging me
The words you hear
Making, stating, concentrating
On aggravating your nerves
And, I judge you
You don't want to be free
You want to be mad
Always sad
Looking for bad in every situation
I've been here with you before
Sittin' in pain is such a bore
Here, I sit
Wishing you would
Work on your shit
When I need to be working on mine

Me, Myself...

Addicted to this world since a little girl
Doing things to keep up and survive
Survive the extinguishing of passion inside
Not doing what I love or, loving what I do
To whom else should thy self be true?
Self
Absent from one mind blinded by ignorance
No connection to the divine
This don't make sense
Withdrawals from the system, blackouts of stress
Silencing heart—but need to confess
Don't want to do this no more—mind is weak
Don't want do this no more—reached my peak
Mental burnout surrounded by defeat
Not doing what I love or, loving what I do
To whom else should thy self be true?
Self
A slave mentality—servant to the world
Program loaded on boys and girls
Craving passion wanting to love what I do
To whom else should thy self be true?
God
Undisciplined will and sociological lies
Dishonoring of spirit three dimensional ties
Me, myself and I

Do what you love, love what you do
To whom else should thy self be true?
Do what you love, love what you do
To whom else should thy self be true?

100 Eyes

100 eyes watching
He left the Bible open
Time is just a concept
Fear is just a token
I'll never give up
Because I'm so driven
What's the point of being
If you ain't living?
Peacock on my path
Raindrops on my face
Life is what you make it
Your flavor is your taste
If music sounds like noise
Something's taking up your space
Open your third eye
Look upon the vision
This road we're meant to walk
Better get busy

Man Creed

I believe in me
Don't care what you see
I believe in the man inside of me
My mind is a weapon
I use it positively
My brother is my brother
Not my enemy
My word is my bond
I am not afraid
I will do my best
For success I am made

II

Love & Pain

Your own mind is a sacred enclosure into which nothing harmful can enter except by your permission.

~Ralph Waldo Emerson

Listen

Spoke to you twenty years ago
Told you back then what I wanted you to know
But you didn't listen
You were the first students I came to teach
I poured words of wisdom
You called it a speech
You don't listen
Like 226 equals 10
Salvation is the price of sin
You think I'm crazy
Crazy, lazy maybe so
This doesn't mean I don't know... what I'm saying
I don't tell you to listen because I'm so smart
I tell you to listen and not make your life hard
This is wisdom
For a thousand thoughts can change the mind
So, can one word create sound
This is food
Food for the morning
Food for the journey
Food for the concerned
Food for the learned
Can you hear me?
Look at your life
Love your wife
Unfold your arms

Stop choosing strife
Feel the vibration, not the feeling
For the moment is passing
Don't miss your healing
Power, people, person, One
Unity, peace, father, Son
Listen

Penmansh **

Everything don't have to be recited
Some stuff just needs to go on paper
Don't need no applause or approval
Just the removal
Of the stain
Writing
On the wall of pain
While trying to remain the same sane
As expected before things changed
How can that be?
You really don't know me
O, the pain of penmanshit burns
You'll understand when it's your turn

Colorblind

The ground is leveled can't you see
The ground is leveled
We're from the same tree—humanity
But, you refuse to accept and believe
The view has changed
But, not your heart
Revival of love you want no part
We've all been called out
You're still choose the dark
Talking in riddles
Division you want to spark
Just because we disagree
Doesn't mean we don't value the same thing
We all want food, love and protection from the rain
You can't draw near
'Cause you were taught fear
Refuse to seek wisdom
From the One who knows
Prefer a nation of anguished souls
Bearing witness to all you see
Your mind encased—iniquity
Hatred
You hate the truth
God has not changed
Love, grace and mercy are still the same

Not forgetting oppression
Has nothing to do with you
The ground is leveled change your view
Or, be left behind

Conscious

You know it's over, why are you still here?
Scared to do something different
The power of fear
I'm the same way waiting on you to move
That'll ease the guilt when I get the blues
Thought this was it
Guess, we didn't think it through
Hell, it's not my fault what was I supposed to do?
This is pathetic… scared of what people gonna say
What I got to lose? Its' my life anyway
Yeah, but you're not ready
Ego—you don't want to betray
Listen to the heart and logic gets in the way
Besides, it's been years why search for peace?
And give up this holding pattern
Where procrastination is the thief
Think you know it all
Judging the way, I choose
I don't have to know anything
I just reiterate your blues
Keeping company with indecision
By default, is how you choose
Clear text in a blind spot
Too afraid to make a move

Sacrifice

Honey, I stayed for the kids
Really, I did
Nothing against you, honeyboo
Once, I saw love wasn't true
I did what many couples do
Chose to live a love untrue
May God forgive how we live
They didn't deserve additional labels
Neither, did I
Didn't want them to answer
The infamous why… did your parent's love end?
Are they still friends?
Just another course of low satisfaction
Know it's the norm not overreaction
I was scorned and devastated
For my dad's return
I forever waited
But, he never ever came back
Turned my blue sky black
Forever,
Then I met you
Decided never to put
My children through
All that hell
Oh, well
I stayed for the kids

Really, I did
Nothing against you honeyboo

Diversity

I am the daughter of mixed race
Mulattos half-breeds whatever the case
Honky, Nigger, Redneck, Spick
Greaser, Spook, Slant-eyes, Jap
Cracker, Faggot, Wetbacks, Fairies
Dikes, Rag-heads, Camel eaters
Freaks, Geeks, Kike, Bible beaters
Thug, Chicken head, Losers, Wimps
The all out Wussy and sorry ass pimp
Where's your place in the melting pot
Diversity an American concept
A catch phrase no doubt
Another acceptable tool of pointing you out
You're different... you don't
Dance, cook, sleep like I do
Something, something
Got to be wrong with you

Burden

Opposing worlds
Can descend you into depression
I've hit a brick wall
Beyond which I cannot go
Intellect is not working
Forgot what I know
How do you distinguish…
Between clinical depression and spiritual crisis?
Allow the truth to reveal your location
Use the negative to overcome the situation
Seek help not hesitation
Leave your burdens at the station

Perversity

I'm not the most religious of these you see
Come and taste what's eating me
My dignity was sold when I was 7 years old
My dignity was sold when I was 7 years old
Child of a pedophile every moment untold
Confession of my pain doesn't heal my soul
I am the daughter of perversity
Born of molestation and gratification
Exploitation and fascination of evil situations
Taught to lie, smoke crack, steal
Shoot mushrooms and lay on my back
Born to whore, so I was told
Back when I was 7 years old
That's when he took my hole
And showed me how to use it
To his friends my dignity was sold
Back when I was 7 years old
I thank God for AIDS
And the age of accountability
Because now I can rest
And make peace with the 7 year old
Taken by the breast
By the beast of lust
Angel of the curse called perverse
The men... they don't come as often

So, I peacefully wait for my coffin
Perversity an excuse
A label for demonic abuse
Of God given sexuality diluted with perversity
A raping of the mind where it hides behind
An awful state of being of seeing
It's for-real the whole of hell revealed
I thank God for AIDS because now I can rest
And make peace with the 7 year-old in the torn dress
Taken by the breast
They don't come as often
So, I peacefully wait for my coffin
My dignity was sold when I was 7 years old
Child of a pedophile every moment untold
Confession of my pain doesn't heal my soul
My dignity was sold when I was 7 years old

Bitches Brew

Teaching me to whore my body in countless ways
Now, the whore I've become feeds his rage
Freaking he called it and bitch was my name
Breaking off a lil' sumpthin' was the line in his game
Do it like this—filling me up with his seed
Soil of fertility, a purpose indeed
Now things have changed
I'm trippin' no doubt
'Cause Jimmie was in place
The night the lights went out
So, I began to hate this sucka
As I grow in my finesse
As wisdom filled my spirit
And milk filled my breast
Ignoring life as if nothing went down
See Jr. is here, but no daddy's around
So, I do it like this
Start freakin' no doubt
Earning my keep
You know what it's about
I do it like that
Ain't that what you said?
Now the idea of freakin'
Messes up your head
But you're playin' for keeps
Now you're for-real

Wantin' to play daddy relax and chill
You taught me to whore my body
To shake my sweet ass
Baby, the woman you want
Is a woman of my past
There's something else to say to you
The wisdom that filled my spirit
Was god running through
So, I started doing like this
Praying no doubt
Earning my keep with a praise and shout
I started doing like that
Ain't that what He said?
Call on me daily and seek to be led
Told me things from a long time ago
Called me by my name and it wasn't whoe
I confessed with my mouth and now I'm saved
I can't hardly remember all the hell that I raised
See, u taught me to whore my body
To shake my sweetness
He taught me to love, forgive
And see that I'm blessed
Because of Him I can talk to you
And pour out that cup of bitch's brew

Bitter

Sour is the inside
Having swallowed a chosen seed
Thoughts of a regretful life
Fearing punishment indeed
Pleasure is no more sin is satisfied
The Game is such a bore
Bitter the taste of pride
This feeding has left me ill
Loyalty to flesh undefined
Unbalanced act of will
Suppressed by the exactness of time

Worrier

Belabors on non-essential matters
Can't control negative talk
Urges to incite conflict
In baggage shoes you walk
Trust in chaos, speaks in haste
Time of others you love to waste
More than nosey, rosy—insecure
Questions you ask, you're so unsure
Like beige
Go ahead get enraged
You can't because you're too afraid
Mind filled with shadows shade
Play actors you factor
You're not true to you
Worried about what people say
Perhaps, getting your due
Stupidity is, stupid you know
Fairness your argument
Keep putting on a show
Poor attempt of persuasion
Better get control of behavior
Worrier, remove the mask and be done
Hunger isn't satisfied by eating a crumb
Unless it's wisdom
Get some

Skeptic

Is God interested in the mess we make?
Risk we take
It's all fate
Right?
So, why be concerned
Have you not learned?
Why do you doubt?
Just figure it out and move on
Can you?
Make the mistake
Show up late
Forget the date
Do the double-take
Be an ingrate
See who cares
It doesn't matter
Chatter
Will always disturb your peace
Escape from you there's no release
Soon enough you'll decease
So, what's the point?
Go smoke a blunt
Whatever you make
Take for your own sake
True love sometimes feels like hate

Skeptic, in what holding pattern
Do you wait?

Coward

I ruffled his feathers
I did
I struck his nerves and got under his skin
If I had a chance I'd do it again
I don't care
My offense was intentional
Like the wind coming off the ocean
The movement of motion
I made my words smooth
Left him an option to choose
The intensity of impact on his mood
I loved it
Face of a startled clown
Words stuck in his throat
Couldn't make a sound
I had him
Took his power
Words hit like a thunder shower
I know the path his mind took
I didn't take time to look
Fooled himself, saw me as impolite
C'mon coward put up a fight
The rules apply to all of us, right?

Lack

Easily recognizable
Personally undeniable
The you I see
Is the shadow side of thee
The place where you go
Thinking nobody will know
What you run your mind through
If, only you had the courage to do
Hanging out in storms
Functioning off of norms
Trying to conform
For others you perform
Suffering from self-defeat
From your plate you cannot eat
Can't accomplish dreams
Because you believe in lack
Position yourself for imaginary attack
Giving off energy your sense can't see
Constant vibration of self misery
On and on and on you go
Where you end up is where you go

Perfectionist

It's hard for me to let you be who you are
Because you're not, who I am
It's hard for me to let you "be"
Who you are
'Cause you do things that make me say "damn!"
Perfection I'm not seeking
This lie I tell myself
It's just that I'm afraid
You'll become someone else
I'll try not to be a stumbling block
But my expectation of you is all I've got
To keep me feeling purposeful
'Cause I've made you
My purpose
And I did it
On purpose
'Cause I couldn't figure out
My purpose
It's hard for me to let you be who I'm not
'Cause expectations of me I have not
But of you
You're my chance to get it right

If

If I knew you, I'd speak
If I speak to you, I'd talk
If I talk to you, I'd listen
If I listen to you, I'd learn
If I learn you, I'd know
If I know you, I'd trust
If I trust you, I'd teach
If I teach you, I'd love
If I love you, I'd need
If I need you, I couldn't be without
And, we don't want that
We want what we see on reality TV
Perception transmitted a billion times
Captions bound in pattern waves of sound
Called communication
This is how we build relationships...

Called

Wanted to tell you something about how I feel
You didn't know
You didn't hear it in my voice
When you answered the phone
I walked around the store feeling like
I should call you back and say
Hey
I wanted to tell you this
But, you were in your world without me
I'm cool though
My stomach aches
But I'll wait
My patience is short
But I'm cool
I just don't know
When you infected me so
And...
I don't like my thoughts of you
Interrupted

Connections

You look at me like I'm beautiful
Staring at me with that inviting grin
Leading me all the way in—into you
The place where you rest, repeatedly confess
Comfortably undress
So, I can see true, true nature of thee
'Cause you want me to know you
Know you well, I can tell
By the time you take to make me comfortable
Giving me a reason to love you
Rearranging your mess
Revealing life of the blessed
All the progress along your journey
How discerning yet, earning of attention
I'm provoked to mention you in my mind
Over and over, time after time
Not coming in out of this rain
There's something I gain
You wet the tip of essence
I long for your presence
You can't turn me off
I want to fit in your pocket
Like your hip in its socket
I must ask, have we met before?
Something I wouldn't deplore

Helping you explore, all you adore
Keeping score, as you look at me like
I'm beautiful, staring at me with an inviting grin
Leading me all the way into you

Tour Guide

Did you know when we met
We would be like this?
Did you know when we met
I'd feel like a familiar kiss?
On your forehead
Helping you, help me through
Clear each other's view
Seeing you in me, and me in you
Did you know it would be so real?
You'd be filled with zeal
To take on what seem like the world
But it's just your payload
Your portion while passing each junction
And learning to function
In this unction, the skin you're in
The one you chose before you came
When you picked your name
And agreed to leave the plane of peace
Did you know?
Did you know you'd want to be released of desire?
Crave a cease of participation
Running around from station to station
Making a mess of things that don't matter
Hearing the chatter sound like clatter
Music of the mad hatter

Between the ears hosting your fears
Drive-by a silent cry and you reply why
To questions you already know the answers to
Did you know I'd be the one to remind you of that?
I'm sure you knew
I'd put food on your plate
Encourage you to take
Another bite of me
For, I am feast of fantasy
More defined than intimacy
A passage, a knowing, a rite of way
Pouring in and out
Deafening of a soft shout
You long to hear over and over again
Whispers of your name by a girl called friend
Who knows where to find you in the end
Because you told her where you'd be
Can you add to me?
Please

Injunction

I'm an injunction
You use to function
A measure by which you define
Part of who you are
Who you are learning by far
A result of growth and time
If you seek approval from me
Who's your authority?
Stratification in mind
Beginning ending of your line
Of identity
An injunction, an authority
What else do you need
A reason to explore
All you want indeed
Desire is not present
It has never been
Desire doesn't exist
Only self and sin

Reason

Something I need
Give me a reason to leave
Where I'm at
Give me a reason to leave
My mind is set
On you
Anyway
Who's says I have to stay
I repeat these cycles
Million times a day
I'm looking for a reason to leave
Just come my way

Pillow-Talk

It's always nice to think of you
How we use to sit what we use to do
If I were there
I'd lay your head on my breast
Pull you close to feel your chest
Hold you tight
'Cause that's what you need
Feel your presence
Listen to you breathe
Close my eyes
Invade your dreams
Rub my feet on yours
Isn't that part of the scene?
Ease your mind a
Numb your pain
Whisper in your ear
What's my name?
Oh, how I miss what we use to do
How we use to sit
Umm... you miss it too

Timing

Thought you'd like to see me
When I look like morning dew
Thought you'd like to see
'Cause you don't get that view
Fire still in eyes from last night's rest
Slumber in my voice as I confess....
I went to sleep
With you on my mind
Woke up to a thought of giving you time
Thought you'd like to see me
When I look like morning dew
But you weren't there when I came through

Chemistry

The flood, rush of chemistry
Impairing judgment and good sense
What a fool in love is full of
Chemistry the ministry of passion

Confession

I position myself awkwardly
For your advancement
Your approval
My lust for you
Is part of the punishment
For my sinful yearnings
Don't you know that?
Like the sap of a rotted Maple tree
Sticky is the faith of your lies,
Sticky is the appetite of my desire

Not Sorry

I knew you could feel this energy
The other level between you and me
Twisted thoughts—perplexity
Double-dipped sameness—humanity
Wrapped in mental tranquility
But you had to let me go
I knew you could feel it
I knew it when you spoke to me
Eyes your smile could not see
An open road laid before me
Exposing all territory
Alpha you owe no apology
For experiencing the other side of surety
Emotions run deep, like an experiment
Shackled at the feet of time never spent
Should haves bought by secrecy with the self
If only another time or, someone else
That's the beauty of being free
Seeing the absolute of thee
Awaking new reality
Opposition, confrontation,
Duality of conversation
Level after level of hesitation
Imagination and shadow situations
Whispers of... I can't help myself
Because I don't want to

The yin in yang we are one—the same
Just the mere mention of name
And I have to catch my grip
Before I slip
Slip and fall and lose it all
All is all I got
Waited so long, so sorry I'm not
But you're not for me
Can't soil the land through misdeeds
Of appetites and bulldog fights with the psyche
Turmoil will spoil a precious thing
Leaving a stain on promise that shouldn't be
Releasing all vulnerability
I knew you could feel this energy
The other level between you and me

Mental -Tution

It's such a delight to engage you
It's such a delight I can't wait too
Connect and infect my mind with you
Project and stretch my thinking too
Move me across the land
Chase me barefoot through mounds of sand
I lose myself… giving up control
Placing my mind in your palms
Where you hold… me gently
Stroking my thoughts
Nourishing my words
Watching dutifully as meanings transferred
Before you release me to journey without you
Mark my memory with your tattoo
Of delight—it's quite right
And I laugh

Habit

You stimulate a part of me that makes me smile
Thought I'd lost you for a while
Am I addicted to you?
I hope so
Addiction is the place where habits grow
I want you to be my habit
Will you be my habit?
Come on baby shoot up my veins
The color of this mix—definitely insane
Wrap me up and watch me sleep
Sit on the edge of the bed and rub my feet
The juices are flowing—got that stomachache
Brain is on pause everything else can wait
They say habit is hell; this is not the case
You motivate me and fill my space
I think of you and write to the stars
Could chill with you even on Mars
See my imagination? Told you it's you
Give me what I need—do what you do
Become my habit
I don't want to become conscious
that changes the rules
a vibe this powerful never want to lose
there is no shame in what I feel
moving beyond this language

no way I can heal
What I'm saying is...
I want you to be my habit

All In

Pull back the covers
Expose the full view
Fear, light and darkness
Inside of you
Who is this person?
How is this so?
From, where did you come?
From, how do you know?
Let me hide, don't call me out
Walk on the edge
Hear my shout
What's happening to me
You have no clue
Like all of our moments
You're just being you

I could

Enlighten my view
Help me see you
Understand hue
Embrace new
Discover true
For, I could love you deeply
Or, run for my life
Either way its movement
Not heaven sent
Really, you make me sick
I move to your tick
Making me forget
Exactly how slick
You really are
Still, I could love you deeply

Kinsman

O, taste and see the experience of Free
Unencumbered by a degree
Travel light perceptibility
I, you, me, we are one
Since the rising of the sun
Kinsman
No longer focusing on cause
Because we live in affects
Call time shared absolute regret
Use the eraser of selective forget
But we cannot
Because I am part of you
You're a part of me
Together we create universally "the whole"
To antagonize a part
Will strike cords in the heart
Of humanity
Leveling understanding
My words are ear candy
Expression of Eve, offspring of Adam
Can you relate, excuse me, madam?
Why oh, why does it make sense to you?
Connection is the cause that affects true
Taking care of me, takes care of you
Kinsman

The Room

Everything I touched
Stimulated me so much
The knob on the door wasn't even a bore
Must've been my love
Everything seemed to fulfill all my dreams
Darkness embraced and kissed my face
Had to have been my love
The open mouth of the chair
Took me there
Cushions pushing back at me
Rocking with some kinda harmony
In a place "called" my space
Every memory I could taste
The smell of comfort locked up in me
Soothing presence of familiarity
The sound of the clock made
My conscious drunk with satisfaction
For a fraction of time can envelope the mind
The room was free the room was me
Knowledge supplied I refuse to hide
The mirror of my love

Water boy

Thoughts of you liquefy senses
Remove defenses
Warmth is lit
Center I sit
Appetite matches tingling vibrations
Smell the fragrance of anticipation
Let's make conversation and relations
Speak without sound
Connect infect and reset time
Become the explosion
Between passion and delight
Liquefy my senses
This feels right

More Than

Creative romantic
More than good
Better than glad
More than excited
Never mad
Mentally wet is your effect
In two minds
Thinking outside lines
Growing like a vine
Continue to water me
I need to grow
You bring something I think I know
Pulse quickens passion thickens
Causing love, hate
Are you a mistake?
Creative romantic
More than good
You're not good for me

Extension

Fake like my hair
He didn't care
Just wanted me there
For one thing
I know how to make him sing
Story of life
Never will be his wife
Plays the same scheme
Learning love wasn't the theme
Pay attention
Body desire held his dream
Did I mention
Fake like my hair
He didn't care
Just wanted someone there

Duped

Sucked into the pain
No idea of the game
Don't know why he asked my name
Or, why I answered
Pulled all the way into the pain
No good intention ever had he
Only the intensity of chemistry
Absorbed him quickly
Invitation to mind never decline
Passion the process of natural design
Dopamine hit my brain exchanged
Only to be left in the rain of pain
Duped—no idea of the game
Why did I ever tell him my name?

Infected

The germ of defeat
Hosted your speech
Actions and behavior
That's why you were not able
To love me properly
For, I am a part of you
You're part of me
Together we create universally
But, you couldn't see
For selfish reason of mind
Your affect destroyed
The balance of design
Dedicated to you
Moments shared are true
I really did love you

Cause 'n Effect

Your affection caused your erection
Which you interpret as love
It's not…it's attraction
Your attraction causes your reaction
Which you interpret as love
It's not…it's emotions
Your emotions cause your devotion
Which you interpret as love
It's not…it's desire
Your desire causes your body fire
Which you interpret as love
It's not… it's temptation
Your temptation creates your situation
Which you interpret as love
It's not… it's sin
The sin of being in the skin
Chosen assignment before life herein
Which we have been told is love
It's not

Headache

You're my headache
I want to be awake
And not think of you
Love was so true
Now, it's blue
Let go, how so, I don't know
For it grows on its own
Even when left alone
Its attended somehow
By thought
Loved, as in past tense
This doesn't make sense
There's no evidence
The imprint on heart
No one will ever see
Much like disease
You're eating me

Turn Down

I really want to turn you down
In my mind
From 1000 to zero
Shut you down not hear your sound
Change you from a verb to a noun
Because you're to active
In my receptor connector
Facilitating my cerebral flow
How I don't know
Like oxygen I breathe you in
Don't know how it began
Don't want it to end
Can't explain it to friend
Don't need to
Its chemistry, history our story
You and me

C Notes

C-notes and painkillers
That's what you are to me
Thorn in my side
My apology
Short story of our time
Possible trilogy
Writing c notes like painkillers
Loves' art fantasy
Like dark chocolate I had you for breakfast
High off chemistry
C-notes and painkillers a warrior's soliloquy
Are you my Shakespearean period?
For, thou bring war and passion to the heart
Depthless to mood becomes colorless art
What do you desire of me?
For, your want should match my request
Need craves your energy silencing mind's unrest
Be music
I'll move to your sound
Become words
I'll write them down
C-notes and painkillers that's what you are to me
Thorn in my side
My apology

Currency

Must release the current situation
It's not healthy for daily meditation
Spiritually, my peace is interrupted—disturbed
Mentally, my thoughts are negative—consistent
Physically, I'm off track—tired
Energetically, I give off bad vibrations—negative
Emotionally, I have episodes—exhausting
Must release the current situation
It's not healthy for my daily meditation

Disqualified

Your quality of love is too low
You look like you need to go
Away
Basic and self-serving
All take and no give
Only on one side do you care to live
Selfish
Balance is required between two
Secrecy and pretense, I cannot do
Really could've loved you
Dummy

Past the Pain

Your effect on me is just not the same
No longer do I hear whispers of your name
In my mind—mind's eye
Something's change, we've changed, I've changed
You've helped me to change
I can no longer respond to you in the way of the past
In this temporal world nothing will last
Not even love, because it's ever changing
Becoming more or, less only we decide
To expose ourselves or, forever hide behind
Brokenness and all the mess that we create
Somehow, I've made the mistake
Of loving you for true
Mistaking grey for blue
Realizing wilderness is a zoo
Where I've caged myself for only your view
Freedom never comes in the physical sense
It's a mental state using every sense of being
Close eyes you'll be seeing—truth of existence
Crushing lies of persistent illusions
Design to create confusion's obvious intrusion
Leading towards change…your effect isn't the same
I've moved past the pain
No longer hear whispers of your name
In my mind—mind's eye

Surging

Highly irritated, full moon
Tide rising be here soon
Be free flood the land
Without warning but, with plan
Destruction, rebirth, earth within
How do I explain the condition I'm in?
I don't
Explanation I do not owe
No one explained Middle Passage or, Jim crow
I need a drank, loosen my tie
Sit and witness, lie after lie
At the bar
Attitude of defiance, reliance on me
Claim and call it personality
Set yours free and you'll see
Tides rise and suns set
Flood the land with no regrets
But, with plan
Highly irritated, full moon
Tide rising be here soon

Requests

Drive me wild as wild could be
Oh, the strength that controls me
When eyes are closed
Love is open wide
Destinations unknown
Please be my guide
Darkness in motion
Rhythm, the moves
Exploring inhibitions
Every ache soothed
Feeling of presence
The intake of breath
Love needs to be loved
For weariness will not rest

Conqueress

Give it to me
I'm gone' take it
Either way I'm gone' break it
'Cause I wanna get into it
Make it mine
See you from the inside
Exploit your mind
Tell you lies
Make you cry
Question your God
Wondering why
Why did she treat me like that?
What's wrong with me?
Nothing, nothing is wrong with you
I just had some conquering to do

Refreshment

I sipped my wine and thought of you
I thought of you and sipped my wine
The word compromise came to mind
Where did it come from?
A voice said, "let it flow"
This was getting all too weird
To just let go
I shook my head to get my grip
To top you off
The wine I again sipped

Tired n' Sweaty

Tired n' sweaty on the inside
Tired and sweaty
Nappy n' dready on the inside
Nappy and dready
But, if you call me I'm ready

For-Play

Saw you looking at me today
Couldn't hide behind your eyes
What your mouth wanted to say
Was I beautiful? Did I look good?
It felt like I looked good
Watching me at the light
Saw you looking at me today
Giving off energy words without say
Rode round the block
Looked through the rearview
Saw you 'cause your friend looked too
Wonder what you were saying
Know it was good
It felt good to be understood
Watched me cross the street—dark eyes
Made my hips come alive
Felt my essence come over me
Perfected my strut so you could see
Could feel you watching
Wanted you to look
'Cause it felt good
It felt good to be understood
It felt good to be understood

AGT (All Good Thoughts)

It's raining again
You're on my mind
Smile on my face
Leaves nothing behind
Smell your air
I love to breathe
Hunger of your eyes
Let me receive
Thunder rolls
This storm no escape
Meaning of it all
Perhaps blind fate
What I know is
Time is opportunity
I'm weaker than I use to be
Okay I'll play along
I don't want you anymore
The key is under the rug
I unlocked the back door
I can't behave craving this mix
Come, see if I can't be fixed
Once again expressing the feel
Just one more chance promise to kneel
Smelling the rain
With you on my mind

Smile on my face
Leaves nothing behind

Suga n' Spice

Sweetness enters his veins
Cultivates the mind
A heart easily captured
Though intricate in design
Feign for me, my presence
My breath becomes your air
Sorrow only knows
A constant state of despair
Faithless about life
Fearful of the unknown
Doubting the Divine
Feeling all alone
Spirit speaks to guide
The outcry of rage
Following deception's voice
The mind chooses a cage
Sweetness is the taste
He loved to have around
Sweetness is the poison
Of a man's breakdown
And… that's what little girls are made of

Let it Die

Sometimes…
Just gotta let it die
Fizzle out
Get flat and tasteless
Then you can throw it away

Finally

Feels good letting go of the rest
Closure an ending phantom love's death
Burial of emotions faded memories
Tied died to the situation
A travesty

III

Seasons

I've done as well as I can, and to think this is part
of the Master's plan. ~Moma

Knowing

Queens just so you know...
God doesn't make you a whoe'
Thought I'd tell you
So, you can let that go

Queen Shoes

I want to say, I don't understand you
I hear what you say and watch what you do
And, I ask myself... what is wrong with you?
I want to say, you make me sick
'Cause the stuff you do to yourself
Don't make sense—but it does
It makes sense and I understand
See, I can sit in judgment and act confused
But, to speak from truth
I must walk in your shoes
What do I understand?
I understand...
When you're trying to fill a void
Or, believe there's something you lack
Anything goes, even a hit f crack
Looking for love in all the wrong places
Trying to feed yourself in-between the spaces
Gaps of time—never having loved defined
I understand and relate to your world
'Cause when I look in the mirror
I see that same sister girl
We all have a past we call history
We're from the same source
So, there's a collective responsibility
See, to lose one is to lose part of the whole

This is the part of the story you were never told
I can stand here and tell you what you need to do
But let me begin by saying, "I'm sorry" to you
God gave you to me and you were a clean slate
What I loaded on you was error and mistake
I'm sorry I left you to be raise by the world
That I let you see me get abused
That I didn't tell you about your sex
Or, how your body could be misused
Taught you how to accept disrespect and infidelity
To look upon your sister as though she was the enemy
I left you looking for a dad that you never knew
Ran away from life and lived a lie in front of you
How to talk loud, fuss and cuss
To be suspicious and never trust
How to be mean and act like a fiend
Place a value on your looks
And build low self-esteem
How to twerk, jerk, shake and sass
But, not how to solve an equation in math class
How to cash a check at Payday Loans
Get yo' hair and nails did and pay yo' cell phone
How to get pregnant and raise babies as a teen
Give up on yourself and let go of your dreams
For, introducing you to crime and low expectation
Allow TV and music to teach you basic education
To hide guns and drugs for you man...call it loyalty
Continuing the cycle of prison and poverty

For, losing our home and having to live on the street
And, depend on you for something to eat
Yeah, I showed you the Bible, but never read what's in it
But, I taught you all of the steps at the abortion clinic
I shoved God down your throat and expected you to pray
Never took the time to talk and teach you how to say, "I'm sorry"
I need to see, you're the better part of me
I need to know you have someplace to go
I need you to try even if it makes you cry
This poem is not about how you feel
You're hearing these words because we need to heal
See, I couldn't love you 'cause I didn't love myself
I thank God for staying with you even though I left
You've got to forgive me to let you pain go
There's something else I want you to know
I've heard the alternative facts
I've seen the fake news
I need you to know
You're walking in Queen shoes
Don't believe the alternative facts
Don't listen to the fake news
I need you to know
You're walking in Queen shoes
So, think 'cause... you're gonna do
Get up 'cause... you're gonna fall
You've got to know who you are

And, believe you're worth it all
Love and respect yourself
You have to choose to lose
Look down at your feet
You're walking in Queen shoes

Fallen Star

Twinkle twinkle rising star
How I wonder who you are
Shine so bright shine so high
A diamond in the father's eye
Twinkle twinkle rising star
The choice is yours, you choose how far
Listen to your heart my dear
Everything you need is there
Take the chance believe in you
Don't stop yourself choose to go through
Challenge yourself, act on your dreams
Rewrite your script if you don't like your scene
You're worth it all, only you can stop you
Even when afraid choose to go through
It's not my assignment to know who you are
This is your "life movie", you are the star
Truth, no one can change what's happened to you
The decision is yours to keep moving through
Move through things that hold you back
Guard your mind, do you believe in lack?
For, there's nothing new under the sun
There's nothing new that can't be done
These words are not just for your generation
Change is the constant state, of a soul's obligation
Because, we are the energy of God

It's not my assignment to know who you are
Just to remind you a queen is a fallen star
Twinkle twinkle the Queen's a star
Do you know who you are?

Woman Crisis

All of this stress and all of this mess
I'm living in a scattered consciousness
I've got, all of this stress and all of this mess
I'm living in a scattered consciousness
As the cancer, eats away my breast
I must confess, I never learned to see
About the woman in me
I learned to sacrifice and give advice
To always be nice and do everything twice
To compromise and wear a disguise
To gossip telling vicious lies
But never, ever celebrate and appreciate
The woman I see...
Looking back at me
With failing health, seeking rest
An enlarged heart lies within her chest
She says...
But what was I supposed to do?
The children needed me and my man did too
So, I... silenced my mentality
Suppressed my sexuality
Accepted infidelity
As so not to challenge masculinity
In a world that ignores the value of "she"
The societal rope around my neck

Has kept me in check
See, I live in a place
Where being feminine is, a disgrace
So, they cover my hair and cover my face
And put me in a space called gender
Where I'm ruled by constant bouts
Of surrender of self
So, you see, Eve is left
With only the social quality
Of the rib that Adam gave to thee
My children are living in a generation
Where foster care is the normal situation
Sex trafficking and prostitution
Often times seem my only solution
I got stiletto heels a pimp and a thong
Exploiting my body using a pole and a song
I'm burning with desire and a need to confess
Mastering lost libido, high blood and stress
Working twice as hard, getting paid for less
I am a WOMAN IN CRISIS
I am "SHE"
Who chooses to be male
I'm on my second marriage
Because the first one was hell
I had my first baby before I was sixteen
And the names they called me
Certainly, wasn't queen
I'm the wife, mother, sister and homemaker

The forgotten daughter locked incarceration
My sisters where are you in this mess
Of gender bias consciousness?
We are living proof of MLK's dream
Pledge with me to walk like a queen
I will think before I do
I will rise each time I fall
Because I am strong and beautiful
Remember I am worth it all
Treat others with respect
Never give up on my dreams
Ask for help and give it
Because I am a queen

Mother

Even when I've loved you less
You've taught me more
The sound of your voice
I could never ignore
For you are my mother
Not brother sister or, family friend
The one who wiped my nose
And held my hand
Thank you
Precious doesn't describe the value of you
Priceless assigns meaning to what you do
Irreplaceable...yeah
Now that's a start
Explaining what you've done to my heart
Even when I've loved you less
You've taught me more
Because you are my mother

The First Sign

Your spirit left me as I walked down the stairs
That was the first sign, the first sign
So, engaged in the chaos of daily life
I tuned in
Spirit said, you don't feel as close as you use to
That's no big deal
A big deal it was
The time you spent sitting alone
In front of the tv
In low energy
That was the first sign, the first sign
The assumption was age
Not some stage
This is how life goes
As we turn the page
We get older, slower
But, you were alone
Inside you knew something was wrong
The time you told me you couldn't
Make it up the hill
That was the first sign, the first sign
When you had to sit more often than stand
Sometimes I hate the master's plan
We buried our head in the sand
That was the first sign, the first sign

The time I spent daydreaming
How much better our lives would be
If I lived near you and you near me
That was the first sign of true
A sign that you needed me and I needed you
In a different way than previous day
A hand, a shoulder
Who knew it would be over
We didn't know how to make it alone
We gave each other strength
We could rely on
But we didn't know
What we had was already gone
We were at the end of our love song
I saw you standing on the sand
In my dream alone
That was the beginning of a life without me
The first sign
The chemo line
The long nights crying
The slow pace of dying
All the while trying
To preserve
The moments
Minutes ticking away
Day by day
For, the last time we'd speak
Without using words

Your voice was the first I ever heard
That was the first sign of life
For me with you
The bottom line of my true love
Oh, how I miss you

Scared

I'm gone say it
I ain't gone lie
I don't want my moma to die
I'm gone say it
I ain't gone lie
I don't want my moma to die
Don't seem right
The way it's going down
I cain't see
Moma not being 'round
I got her hands
Got her feet
Humor heart
Even the position I sleep
Cook like her, act about the same
Use my left hand to write my name
Don't seem right
The way it's going down
I cain't see
Mama not being 'round

Just the Facts

Survival is low
We've entered stage 4
Miracles come and go
And, we don't know
What the hell we're doing
But we're doing it
All chipping in
Fearing the end
How do I begin to say…
Even in your sleep
You were able to teach
Faithfulness, acceptance and love
You were able to
Because it wasn't about us
It was about you
All of the pain
You'd been living through
Even as a sleeper
You're still our teacher
I love you

Levels

Its deeper than we know
I've been shown this for show
We become less of ourselves
The more we grow
Into who we really are

Witching Hour

We've entered the witching hour
What a quiet time it is
We've enter the witching hour
Where the battle is really His
As we stand on the promises
Awaiting deliverance
We have not forgotten
The witching hour it is

Silence

I need the silence so, it can run its course
Silence teaches me to seek
The me I cannot reach
Through the awakening of the self
Where God has left or, where I have
Left God
Isn't that odd
In the silence I hear
Rage is quite near
Crying out in fear
Of me letting go of him
In silence I think
About what I just ate
All the mistakes—lesson of my fate
Seeing myself or, what is left
Oh, tattered soul, full of secular holds
How I love thinking I'm in control
Silence
Silence teaches me to seek
The me I cannot reach
Through the awakening of the self
Where God has left or, where I have
Left God

Dance

She wasn't given a chance
To do her dance
To walk around and prance
Or, take a stance
Against anything
So much pride was in her voice
When she said, "I lost five pounds"
She'd really done something for herself
For the first time...this moment is mine
I forgot to mention
The disease hadn't got her attention
It hadn't played its hand
But, we'd entered the land of sickness
All witnesses but, didn't know
To whom did we owe it?
How do you grow it?
But not show it...until
Stolen delight ended up in a fight
For what's called life
More than the strife of being
Mother, sister, friend, wife
Someone rolled the dice
Cut deeper than a knife
Exposing how short life
Really is

Walking around the track
Unknowingly under attack
Trying to get back some of what she'd lost
But paying the cost
The game had been played
Fat lady was on the stage
When we showed up
Dice rolled, her story told
Expiration of her soul
Now events must unfold
As she walked around the track
A bead of sweat rolled down her back
The expected chance of being able
To do her dance
Walk around and prance
Even take a stance had expired
Pulled from the shelf
All of us left witnesses
In the land of sickness
Damn…

Watchmen-

I have no desire for sex
for sleep
to talk
to seek
I only want to be still
Still and listen to you
Without words
As you're going through
Like the movement of the ocean
Doesn't acknowledge time or, devotion
Transition a language without speech
No desire for sex, talk or, sleep
Watchmen, watchmen, please leave
Without her I cannot breathe

Suddenly

Clouds roll across the plains
Eruption of volcano
Softness of rains
Let me listen
Spirit needs to write
Something tells me
The end's in sight
I sit I listen
Hear the rise of your breath
For there, I'm at peace
Suddenly your souls at rest

Exits

Mouth, nose, ears and all the holes
Mouth, nose, ears and all the holes
Windows, doors, stairways, floors we use them
No matter the path of escape
Spirit chooses a destined fate
A portal… a gate to exit
As it enters it must also leave
Absence of presence is why we grieve
However, we must celebrate
Celebrate a time of knowing
Of letting go
Exits are inevitable
Each has its own
Live what you know
Not here for long
Exits monitor the pace of time
You'll never lose your place in line
Mouth, nose, ears and all the holes
Windows, doors, spaces, floors we use them

Darkness

Darkness sits upon my head
It was all in my bed
I woke up this morning
Remembering the dead
What momma said
I really love bread and oil
Grind everyday call it toil
Fresh bitter is the mist
My brother I truly miss
Not everyone will capture this
'Cause we're all not that deep
Many still asleep
Do you know if you're awake?
Do you believe in fate?
Are some deaths a mistake?
Gone too soon
Gloom and emptiness in full bloom
I feel time but can't keep the pace
Sadness and depression has a taste
You look and ask me what's wrong
Someone I truly love is gone
But this isn't your time zone
I'm here with my new friend Alone
World empty without you
Keep asking myself what am I going do
Know the lord will see me through

But that's not something
I wanna do… right now
Never ever
Say it'll get better
Tears are wetter
Keep falling behind
All off my grind
Mind keeps talking
Don't like this view
This is more than missing you

Long Quiet

Long quiet, quiet long
Long quiet, quiet long
It's been quiet for a long time
It's been long for a quiet time
It's been a quiet time for long
Leaves fallen
Seasons changed
So much to where
It'll never be the same
Tree uprooted not cut down
Pulled from mother earth
She groans at the sound
Pain—
Absence, presence and rebirth
No longer physical on this earth
Planted elsewhere growing green
In the garden a new world
Behold the scene
Overcome by joy in which she sees
Peace, love, familiarity
Long quiet, quiet long
It's been quiet for a long time
It's been long for a quiet time

Spring's Here

Sun shines upon face
Basking in the wonderment of grace
Oh, how I long to see your face
I miss you
Can't believe it's been almost a year
Can't believe your no longer here
Somehow, I wonder if you are near
I miss you
I can't stand noise
So, I keep it quiet
Listen way beyond the riot
I want to hear you
Speak to me, I think
But what does that mean
I wish you again
Were a part of my scene
Sometimes I don't know
What the hell it all means
I just miss you

Bridges

Crossover bridge to me
Mother is a tree
I feel her energy
Reconnect
To what you can't see
I've crossed a bridge
It leads to me
Petals off my flower
New buds enter light
Pathway to me
Always been in sight
Seeing beyond perception
Joy akin delight
Take the time to find
Your own guiding light

Thirsty

Me, you, a glass of water and the good Lord
Gone' go upstairs
First, I'm gonna ease my mind wit' a shower
'Cause when I stop movin'
Its pounding by the hour
Thoughts—good, bad, majority sad
Self-loathing, unfolding, rapidly mad
'Bout how life, one given to me
A book of instructions of how I'm supposed to be
Mastering appetite and turning the other cheek
Not being of this world from which I seek
All pleasure
How do you measure or, draw the line?
Between the soul of man and spirit of Divine?
Somehow, they merge often a clash
Like, the water poured in my glass
Before, I came upstairs
Me, you, a glass of water and the good Lord
Gone' go upstairs
To go downstairs in my mind
Down to a place where I spend most time
Contemplating, desperately waiting, seeking Divine
Show up, show out
That's what the church shout
Wait with faith renew strength

Endure all things reach zenith
Me u a glass of water and the good Lord
Gone' go upstairs
To go downstairs in my mind

Contact

Ever felt beauty without touching a thing?
Ever felt power the kind energy brings?
Ever been present without being there?
I have
Difficult to understand
Because the mind has limits
Difficult to imagine
If you've never been in it
The presence of beauty
Without looking upon
The warmth of magnificence
Knowing you're with the One
This is not love
This is something beyond
The mind can't conceive
Logic so overdone
Experience and receive
A matter of fact
You cannot ignore
When you've made contact
Please visit me again

Being

Kingdom of God lives in me
Part of me you cannot see
Writing what I think, dream
How I feel
Being with me is how I heal
Not concerned with the outcome
Inner teacher speaks to me
Learned to listen so, you can see
Spirit responds to the inner man
You can do all things he can

Drumbeat

Why are you still asleep my child?
Why do you sleep, I say?
Don't you hear the drumbeat of your heart?
The chariot comes this way
I am not here to guide
Or, give wisdom that will last
I am here to feed your soul
Lay pillows along your path
This food comes from the spirit
One you cannot deplete
But you must receive
So, rise—get on your feet
Everything I am, I give it all to you
All that you become
Is your illusion of what is true
Forget about the physical
For, it is but a host
The mirage of the external
Is where you sleep the most
Time is not the enemy
Nor, is it a friend
It simply marks an entrance
Also, the end
Why are you still asleep my child?
Why do you sleep, I say?

Follow the beat—rise to your feet
The chariot comes your way

Children

You may not know what to do
Just remember God's got a plan for you
Think of all the things you've been through
Reading these words from me to you
Don't worry about the decisions ahead
Thank him daily and seek to be led
I know there were times
When you wanted to quit
When the thought of continuing
Really made you sick
Look at all you've gained
Lessons you'll continue to learn
It's not about what you do
But who you'll become
I can't tell you about living
But, I can tell you about life
Everything is temporary
Even happiness and strife
Jobs, cars and material things
You'll go through as you chase dreams
When you look up and see no way out
Continue moving, have no doubt
Faces going places many have never been
Plant seeds, open doors with the wind
Go in peace, travel light and choose well

Be kind to everyone your plan will not fail
Because it's not your plan
You're just a vehicle you see
Much like these words to you from me

Self-Hack

I cracked the code
To understanding me
My brain is so excited
I feel sleepy
It's a beautiful new reality
Reconnecting
You can't understand
Because your brain is dead
But you're in body
Feeling like nobody and everybody
That everything's unfair
You can't experience doing
Because your mind is trapped there
Where?
In your chosen house of pain
Be it shame or, fame it constantly rains
Answers to the name you gave it
Wishing someone would help you carry it
But they can't
You own it, can't loan it
Some of you think this piece is deep
Others know this is why you can't sleep
Troubled, under rubble and rubbish
Wondering why exist?
Where's the road to bliss?
Missing the pleasure of ignorance

A time when things didn't matter
You could stand the chatter
Believed in dreams was open to change
Somehow, sun turn to rain
I cracked the code
To understanding me
My brain is so excited
I feel sleepy
It's a beautiful new reality
I'm scratching my itch
Finally

Enhancement

I'm not advanced
Wisdom enhanced
By spirit
Can always hear it
Keep counsel
Stay near it

Free me from the mental bondage of ego, emotional bondage of fear, and conditional illusions of control I choose daily.

This is my prayer.

DeBro

ada

About the Author

De'Broada, is a featured spoken word poet at community events throughout Kansas. She performs spoken word poetry to form connections between the audience and the madness experienced in life. Her wise and prolific expression of poetry help many find a path to healing. The conversational tone of thought provoking pieces explores the many facets of perception and the deep work of becoming self-aware. Illuminating the rhetoric replaying in our mind, she reminds us that storms and obstacles in life are unavoidable, but we are not alone. She believes, all experiences are worthy of creative expression and words are vehicles of power that can inspire action and healing. In her words, "The way I see it, life is training and poetry, empathetically helps make the point that everyone is in the process of interpreting life."

She is also the author of Purple Dark Poetry and, My Way: Finding My Way Back to Me (iCreativ Books 2017).

Follow her:
Facebook @iCreativProperti or, www.icreativproperti.com